KV-511-566

Twin Tricks

by Alison Hawes
Illustrated by Sandie Sonke

Viv   Jess

OXFORD
UNIVERSITY PRESS

Jess and Viv are twins. They look very alike. In fact, people often muddle them up. So, when they go to school, they usually wear different coloured hairbands and jackets. They also take different coloured lunch boxes. That way, people know which twin is which.

Viv wears a blue hairband and jacket and has a blue lunch box.

Jess has a red jacket and a red box.

One day, the twins decide to play a trick on their friends and swap hairbands, jackets and lunch boxes.

"Everyone will think I'm you and you are me," giggles Jess, putting on Viv's coat.

"It's a <u>perfect</u> plan!" says Viv.

So when Jess <u>leads</u> the way into school, no one notices they have swapped – except their teacher!

What is the <u>perfect</u> plan the twins come up with?

Miss Webb grins at the twins.

I will not tell!

Jess <u>leads</u> the way. Does this mean that she is in front of Viv or behind her?

Jess thinks that pretending to be Viv is going to be fun. However, she has to sit next to Viv's best friend, Avril. She wishes she could sit next to her own best friend, Sam, as usual. Sam is always <u>interested</u> in the same things as her. She wonders what Sam is doing.

Jess and Sam are <u>interested</u> in the same things.
What are you most <u>interested</u> in?

Sam is next to Viv.

Viv also thinks that pretending to be Jess is going to be fun. However, she wishes she could sit next to her own friend, Avril, as usual. Avril is always interested in the same things as her.

I miss Avril.

I miss Sam.

At lunch time, the twins open their lunch boxes.

"Yuck! I don't like this food!" they say.

"Oh dear," thinks Miss Webb, "I expect the twins will be hungry. Neither of them looks as if they're going to eat very much!"

Viv has a bit of melon.
Jess has six carrot sticks.

"Is there a <u>reason</u> why you look so unhappy?" asks Miss Webb.

"Yes!" says Jess. "I am fed up of pretending to be Viv. I like being *me* best."

The <u>reason</u> the twins look so unhappy is because they are fed up of pretending to be each other. Can you think of a <u>reason</u> why they prefer being themselves?

Viv is fed up as well.

13

"I like being *me* best, too," says Viv.

So the twins swap hairbands and lunch boxes again.

"Is that better?" asks Miss Webb.

"We thought it would be a <u>perfect</u> plan, but it wasn't," says Jess.

"Will you be swapping again?" asks Miss Webb.

The twins' answer is a big loud …

The twins thought their trick would be <u>perfect</u>. Can you remember all of the things that were not <u>perfect</u> about pretending to be each other?

Read the words

Jess

Viv

well

will

box